Published by OH!
20 Mortimer Street
London W1T 3JW

Disclaimer:
This book and the information contained herein are for general
educational and entertainment use only. The contents are not claimed to
be exhaustive, and the book is sold on the understanding that neither the
publishers nor the author are thereby engaged in rendering any kind of
professional services. Users are encouraged to confirm the information
contained herein with other sources and review the information
carefully with their appropriate, qualified service providers. Neither the
publishers nor the author shall have any responsibility to any person
or entity regarding any loss or damage whatsoever, direct or indirect,
consequential, special or exemplary, caused or alleged to be caused, by
the use or misuse of information contained in this book.

ISBN 978-1-91161-088-5

Editorial consultant: Sasha Fenton
Editorial: Victoria Godden
Project manager: Russell Porter
Design: Ben Ruocco
Production: Freencky Portas

A CIP catalogue record for this book is available from the British Library

Printed in China

10 9 8 7 6 5 4 3 2 1

the little book of
MEDITATION

beleta greenaway

CONTENTS

WHAT IS MEDITATION?

Meditation is a practice in which you concentrate on a specific sound, thought or action. This procedure will help you to control your brain activity and your awareness of the world around you and allow you to reach a state of mental clarity and calmness. In turn, this will improve your spiritual wellbeing. Once you achieve the meditative state, your mind will become clear and focused, allowing you to separate yourself from your earthly surroundings. Successful meditation requires you to be inwardly still and for the brain to become silent. At the same time, it also remains awake and aware, allowing for genuinely creative and inspired thinking.

"The goal of meditation isn't to control your thoughts; it's to stop letting them control you."

Anonymous

CHAPTER

1

the
HISTORY of
MEDITATION

Meditation has a long history.
We associate it with Buddhism today,
but several religions have practised
it, probably since the dawn of time. It
calms the mind, removes us from daily
life and allows us to tap into our own
inner consciousness.

Still, for some people, it also allows
them to connect to their gods for
enlightenment. Meditation has long
been used for its many health benefits
as well as its spiritual ones, but one of
the most wonderful things about it is
that you don't need to meditate alone,
as you can get together with a group
of like-minded friends and meditate in
peace as a group.

*"Meditation is
a silent heart,
a peaceful mind
which can make life
more loveable, more
liveable."*

Anonymous

in the EAST

Many Indian religions have for centuries used the practice of meditation, such as Hinduism, Jainism and Sikhism. There is wall art in India dating back over 3,000 years, showing figures sitting in the lotus position with their eyes closed, which suggests they were practising meditation even then. Similarly, in other beliefs, such as Buddhism and Taoism, meditation is an essential part of the ritual, and, it is believed to have started as far back as the sixth century BC. From Persia came the Bahá'í faith, where meditation is the fundamental principle and the primary way of developing spirituality.

in the WEST

Historically, the Catholic religion encouraged priests, monks and nuns to meditate. However, this was usually described as contemplation, which for them was a form of prayer that would improve spiritual wellbeing and develop greater wisdom.

The non-Christian meditation encourages the mind to be empty. In contrast, Christian traditions were used to focus on biblical topics.

ALTERNATIVE BELIEF SYSTEMS

In other cultures, such as Shamanism and Neo-Pagan faiths, practitioners use meditation to put themselves in an altered state of consciousness.

This enables them to engage with higher entities and to escape their physical bodies. Sometimes, they would do this with the help of hallucinogenic plants, and they would also dance to loud, hypnotic music.

*"Within you is
a stillness and a
sanctuary that you
can retreat to any time
and be yourself."*

Anonymous

CHAPTER

2

MEDITATION
TODAY

In recent times, meditation has become much more widely used, and it has become trendy in many societies as a stress-management technique that is known to improve health and wellbeing.

By reducing emotional stress levels and anxiety, meditation can help people avoid harmful or inappropriate thought patterns. In this way, meditation has an undeniably positive effect on our mental health and can be a great help in times of trouble.

"Meditation is all about the pursuit of nothingness. It's like the ultimate rest. It's better than the best sleep you've ever had. It's a quieting of the mind."

Hugh Jackman

WHY MEDITATE?

People meditate for many reasons. Historically, it was for religious or spiritual reasons, and the intention was for the practitioner to move away from day-to-day issues and lift their thinking to higher thoughts, thereby improving their spirituality.

In the Western world, our focus is very much concerned with the physical world, with little emphasis on looking deeper within our own minds, so we end up having to take care of our mental wellbeing as well as our general health.

CREATIVITY

By looking inside the mind, people such as writers, sportspeople and musicians, often find meditation to be an aid to inspiration.

Writer's block, for example, can be lifted by calming down and allowing the unconscious part of the creative mind to become active.

Similarly, inventors used the same techniques to brainstorm insoluble problems, enabling them to find inspiration for their inventions.

REDUCE STRESS

The world is becoming ever more stressful, and many people find they are continually anxious and uneasy. Sufferers report feeling locked in by the worries of their everyday life and unable to find relief.

By meditating, people can block out these niggling thoughts and find the place of peace.

MINDFULNESS

Mindfulness has been recognized as a great aid to mental wellbeing. Strictly speaking, it is the awareness of something – while meditation encourages the perception of nothing.

The human mind finds it virtually impossible to think of nothing, so the way to get close to nothingness is to focus the mind on simple, non-troubling elements, such as rhythmic breathing or a simple sound.

CLEAR THE MIND

Here is a simple example of how difficult it is to think of nothing. Years ago, when I was being taught meditation, my teacher said,

> *"Whatever you do,*
> *don't think about a yacht*
> *with red sails."*

Needless to say, that image was the first to come to mind, and I had to work hard to focus on wiping it away.

For the mind to filter out the things it does not need, we must condition it to focus on simple, non-troubling elements, such as rhythmic breathing or a pure sound.

Many people will play a recording of "white noise" or gentle music, especially at night, but even the sound of a small desk fan can help.

BENEFITS
of MEDITATION

Meditation is excellent for reducing stress levels and being able to control and lessen the effects of anxiety. It can enhance emotional health by improving self-image and promoting a positive outlook.

Scientifically, meditation can bring down blood pressure and help the heart to have a healthier rhythm. Also, it can encourage self-awareness, enabling the user to acknowledge any negative thoughts or noisy and unhelpful internal dialogue, which reduce self-worth and confidence.

Indeed, it has been noted that meditation encourages kindness, not only to others but also to ourselves.

SLEEP SWEET

There are acknowledged health benefits in the way meditation has been seen to improve the quality of sleep. Conducting a simple contemplation at night before dropping off to sleep can leave you feeling refreshed and renewed the following day.

Simply concentrate on your breathing as you drift into sleep and visualize pretty places in your mind's eye.

"Meditation is being in tune with our inner energy source."

Anonymous

CHAPTER
3

PHYSICAL HEALTH

In medical use, meditation has been found helpful in controlling chronic pain, either by allowing the patient to rise above the discomfort or to change their relationship to their aches and pains.

Those who perform this practice regularly say they manage their ailments with just the power of the mind.

"Meditation is the tongue of the soul and the language of our spirit."

Anonymous

PAIN-RELIEF VISUALIZATIONS

A recognized pain relief technique for the sufferer is to visualize what the pain looks like, and then use the power of the mind to manipulate it. When relaxing, the patient focuses attention on the size, colour and shape of their pain.

For example, if the pain is seen as being bright red, symbolizing heat, then the sufferer can cool it with imaginary ice.

Alternatively, the sufferer may decide to change a vivid red pain to a soft candy pink one, which is a calmer and less abrasive shade.

If the visual image is spiky (a typical representation of sharp pain), the patient can imagine the spikes being smoothed down. The idea is that by seeing the pain in an alternative way, it encourages the mind to react to it differently.

CHANGE your TERMINOLOGY

It is a common concept in treating pain to look at the terminology and wording used in order to amend perception. For example, a patient may be asked to consider an ache as a tingling sensation rather than a painful discomfort. Similarly, a chronic ache may be described as heaviness or throbbing. The generally accepted principle is that some forms of chronic pain cannot be removed. Still, the way they are considered can make it easier for the patient to accept the situation.

To paraphrase William Shakespeare:

"It is not what happens to the man that affects him, but how he feels about what happened."

A well-known tenet in meditation is that accepting our own imperfections is a way of obtaining an improvement in a non-judgemental way.

By acknowledging that we are all flawed but capable of change, we can sometimes ease addictions, and by removing blame and encouraging self-forgiveness, many people change their ways and move on to better lives.

In spiritual terms, to suffer pain makes a person more robust and more able to empathize with the suffering of others.

A saying goes:

*"You cannot teach
what you haven't learned."*

Although mankind dislikes pain, it is said to develop character. On a mental level, practising meditation can train the mind towards self-control and self-confidence, and that can help those who are sick and in pain.

HYPNOTHERAPY HELPS!

My husband, John Greenaway, is a qualified clinical hypnotherapist and NLP practitioner, and he had a female patient who was very ill.

She was suffering from five fatal illnesses at once and could have died at any time. Two or three times, critical surgeries were cancelled at the hospital because her blood pressure was too high for them to operate, and this was happening due to her increasing levels of anxiety.

Eventually, a team of six doctors was assembled to perform the surgery.

A week before this was to happen,
my husband spent five sessions with the
lady, teaching her a meditation technique
that enabled her to focus on bringing
her blood pressure down. At last, it
started to work.

On the day of her surgery, her first blood
pressure reading was still somewhat
high, so she asked the doctor to give her
twenty minutes to meditate. Soon after,
the doctor was surprised to find that
her second blood pressure reading was
normal. The surgery went ahead and was
a complete success.

It has been noted that meditation affects the way our brains work, and specifically, we can lengthen our attention spans quite dramatically. There is also improvement in memory capacity, retention and recovery from illness or operations. Even age-related memory loss can be decreased by prolonged use of meditation.

In the next section, we'll see how the scientific studies of meditation confirm these benefits.

What science says about meditation

A recent study by the University of California, Los Angeles (UCLA) has shown that people who had meditated for twenty years or more had a higher brain volume than those who had never meditated at all! It seems that the long-term effects of meditation increase a person's brainpower.

When they looked at older people who meditated, these people did show some loss of brain volume compared to younger people who meditated regularly, but the difference between them and people who did not meditate was seen to be quite considerable.

Interestingly, the extra volume of brain density is seen across all areas of the brain.

A Yale University study found that mindfulness meditation reduced activity in the part of the brain associated with worrying about the future. It was suggested that this kind of meditation encouraged the practitioners' minds to form new connections, which enabled them to worry less and to dream up better futures for themselves.

CHAPTER

4

DIFFERENT TYPES of MEDITATION

If you thought there was just one kind of meditation, this chapter shows that there are several: some ancient and others more modern. Some have grown out of religious practices, and others have grown out of psychology, mediumship and even hypnotherapy.

"The quieter you become the more you can hear."

Anonymous

VIPASSANA

The ancient Indian teacher, Buddha, is said to have discovered this kind of meditation nearly three millennia ago and taught it as a panacea for all ills.

Vipassana, meaning *to see things as they really are*, aims to concentrate on the connection between the mind and body, bringing a sense of balance and harmony to the soul.

Fully understanding how life has moulded you, how you have grown, where you have failed and how you have suffered, brings enlightenment and encourages you to free yourself from suffering. It helps to increase self-control and to remove delusions, enabling you to reach a state of peace and tranquillity.

CHAKRAS

Another Indian practice involves working with the chakras, the seven centres of spiritual power in the body.

The chakras include the root chakra, the sacral chakra, the solar plexus chakra, the heart chakra, the throat chakra, the third-eye chakra and lastly the crown chakra.

The chakras start with the root chakra at the base of the spine, moving upwards to the sacral chakra, located just below the navel. The solar plexus chakra is positioned under the rib cage and the heart chakra is centred over the heart area.

The throat chakra is located roughly where the Adam's apple is, and the third-eye chakra is located in the middle of the forehead, between the eyebrows.

Lastly, the crown chakra is at the very top of the head, where the plates of the skull are joined.

Each of the chakras is associated with a different colour, and each represents a separate energy force. Each energy force works on the spiritual, emotional and physical aspects of the person.

An energy force called *qi* or *prana*, which is said to be the life force, flows through the body via the chakras.

As different issues can cause this energy to be blocked in the body, meditation can be used to release and clear the blocked energy from the chakras.

YOGIC MEDITATION

Transcendental Meditation, a type of yogic meditation, is another traditional Indian technique. The practitioner uses meditation to rise above the current physical state to achieve enlightenment.

Typically, users recite a repeated phrase as a focus that will help them reach the required state of relaxation.

The repeated phrase is called a mantra.

Some people focus on the sound of "*Om*", and intone it in a long, drawn-out way to produce a rhythmic sound that is quite hypnotic.

Other people may chant "*Om Mani Padme Hum*", which is commonly used in Tibetan Buddhism. You can check out these chants on YouTube.

GUIDED MEDITATION

Here, a leader guides a group of people through meditation. An example may be of the leader telling the students to imagine themselves walking into a wood, wandering along the path until they find a small lake. The lake is filled with the items they may need to increase their spiritual awareness and knowledge, so they must walk into its crystal-clear waters and pick up any of the things that they find particularly useful. Finally, the students walk back out of the lake, along the path and into the world once again.

the CONSCIOUS MIND

There are two components to the human mind: the conscious and the unconscious mind.

The conscious mind deals with the practicalities of life, including feelings, beliefs and memories. This can include harmful elements, such as fears, anxieties and prejudices – and especially sad memories that are left over from childhood.

the UNCONSCIOUS MIND

Sometimes referred to as the subconscious, the unconscious mind includes memories, feeling, motivations and thought processes that we are not consciously aware of and which are subliminal.

It is the source of our automatic thoughts, beliefs, hidden desires and dreams.

So, for example, a person may be *consciously* aware of having a phobia of being at sea, but he does not know why. By searching in the *unconscious*, he might find a repressed memory from early in his childhood, when he fell into a river and swallowed a lot of water, thus becoming extremely frightened. This kind of thought is outside our rational thinking and our day-to-day lives, so there isn't much we can do to control it.

The aim of meditation is to bring order to our thinking by understanding the impact of the unconscious mind and how we can go about managing it.

WAVES

The brain produces both theta and alpha waves while we are meditating.

Under normal circumstances, theta waves occur when we are asleep. When meditating, the fact these waves are present at all shows that meditating induces the kind of brain activity that happens when we are in our most relaxed state or asleep.

CHAPTER
5

HOW to
MEDITATE

The purpose of meditation is to go beyond the limitations of day-to-day thoughts and reach our true nature. This is a state of peace and harmony within us that some describe as a state of bliss or of nirvana, or being at one with ourselves and the universe.

The difficulty is that the mind does not always follow instructions or stay focused, so many of us find random thoughts suddenly springing into our minds. Still, meditation can help us to control and prevent these mental interruptions, or at least limit them.

"Empty your mind, be formless, shapeless – like water. Now you put water into a cup, it becomes the cup, you put water into a bottle, it becomes the bottle, you put it in a teapot, it becomes the teapot. Now water can flow or it can crash. Be water, my friend."

Bruce Lee

RELAX

Traditionally, meditation was performed sitting cross-legged in the lotus position, but this is not necessary. Those who are no longer young and agile can find this uncomfortable, even for short spells. Instead, you should choose a relaxing position, which may be on the bed, sitting in a chair or even standing.

A QUIET SPACE

Importantly, before starting, remove any possible causes of irritation. Ensure that all phones are switched off; alarms are cancelled and tell family and friends not to disturb you for a while. You need external peace and quiet if you are to find internal peace.

Try to find the quietest place, so if you live in a noisy area, I suggest you play some relaxing music or some sort of white noise to blot out the external noise pollution. You may want to cover yourself with a warm blanket in case you feel the cold.

RYTHMIC BREATHING

Breathe from your diaphragm.
It may seem a little odd for a
while, but soon your breathing
will find its own rhythm, and it
will become smooth and even,
thereby calming your mind and
body. Focus your attention on
your breathing.

The 4-7-8 method is a technique that helps to turn your mind inwards and encourage it to block out thoughts and keep you centred.

Slowly breathe in through the nose for a count of four, hold the breath for a count of seven and slowly breathe out through the mouth for a count of eight.

Keep repeating this cycle, focusing on breathing. For the first ten breaths, try to take the air deep down into your lungs. From then on, keep the counts going, but return to more natural breathing.

Start to notice how the breath feels slightly cooler as you breathe in and slightly warmer as you breathe out, because your body will have heated the air while it was inside you.

Take the time to make the time! It is common for mundane thoughts, to come into your mind, such as:

"Did I remember to...?"

"What should I do about...?"

In meditation, you might be aware of these trivial thoughts, but you must try to dismiss them. Just accept they exist and visualize yourself moving them to an imaginary folder on the computer. Place all unwanted thoughts into the folder and tell yourself:

"I will deal with that later."

CHAPTER

6

the
BODY
SCAN

The body scan technique is most useful when you want to relieve stress, and this can be combined with the breathing methods that I mentioned earlier.

Sitting or lying comfortably, focus your attention on your toes, tense them up and then let them go while imagining all the muscles and nerves relaxing. A warm or slightly numb sensation will begin in those parts.

Move the focus to the soles of your feet
and continue the relaxation.

Concentrate on your calf muscles, tense
them and then relax them before moving
on to the thigh muscles, which you should
then also tense and relax.

Take as much time as needed on each
part of your body before you take the
next step.

Imagine your hips and pelvis relaxing before moving on to your abdomen area. Often a lot of stress is stored here, so extra time may be necessary to eradicate the tension completely in the tummy area. Tense your muscles and hold the tension for a moment, and then relax.

Keep breathing rhythmically and deeply, and don't let the mind wander. Mind control is the key to success.

Next, focus on your spine and the muscles either side of your back, tensing and relaxing as the emphasis moves up your body. Concentrate on wrapping the relaxation around the whole top of your body before returning to the shoulder area, another place where stress gathers.

Take time to tense and then relax the shoulder muscles, and feel the tension being soothed away.

When you are ready, focus on the neck and scalp, before screwing up and then relaxing the face muscles and the jaw.

Progressively concentrate your attention on the body and, travelling upwards, gradually tense and relax each part until you reach the top of your head.

If there are any areas of discomfort, ask your mind to send healing energy to those parts.

Making progress

Whatever you do,
don't give in.
Practice makes perfect!

Practise this form of meditation regularly.
The important thing is to keep going
and, eventually, you will see and feel the
benefits. Bear in mind that it's like sowing
a seed: you are not likely to see the
effects immediately; it will take time.

Once you have mastered the art of meditation, you will begin to feel more relaxed in general, and you will have fewer feelings of stress and anxiety. Situations which might have gripped you previously will still be noticeable, but they will have less impact.

The calmness and stillness will become your standard response, and you will have a greater acceptance of life around you.

"For breath is life, and if you breathe well you will live long on earth."

Sanskrit proverb

CHAPTER
7

AIDS to MEDITATION

It is usual for people to use monotonous, relaxing music to create a better focus; this forms a relaxing background that can drown out everyday noise. It is important to find music that is calm and gentle, that keeps a constant pace.

There is plenty of meditation music on the market that you can buy or download for this purpose.

"Meditation brings wisdom; lack of meditation leaves ignorance. Know well what leads you forward and what holds you back, and choose the path that leads to wisdom."

Buddha

SINGING BOWLS

Singing bowls are brass bowls or sometimes even rose quartz bowls, and the way to make them sing is to run a special pestle around their inside edge. This creates one continuous note or tone.

These meditations are usually performed in a group, but you might want to do this as part of a private appointment with a trained professional. Often, the leader will let you record your session, so you can use the ringing tone again later. Some practitioners have the recordings available for you to buy.

GONG BATHS

Other practitioners may use tympani, such as gong baths, as a form of meditation. The vibrations made can resonate with the soul, pulsing through the whole body.

The gongs vary in sizes and provide a reverberation that blanks out their surroundings and allows the mind to be free. People who have this experience often go on to buy their own gongs.

AROMATHERAPY

A meditation that brings excellent results is lying in a warm scented bath. It is best to do this in the evening so that you can go straight to bed afterwards.

Aromatherapy oils help in creating the right mood and frame of mind, while suitable background music can also help.

Important note

Never use essential oils directly on the skin; first, dilute a few drops of essential oil in a little carrier oil such as olive or avocado oil.

DIFFUSERS

You can put a little undiluted essential
oil into a pottery infuser. The infuser
has a space inside for a tealight candle,
and a small dish on top for the essential
oil, which releases its aroma around the
room when the candle is lit and the dish
grows warm.

SPRAYS
and BATHING

Here is another idea. Take a small spray bottle, fill it with warm water, adding three or four drops of the essential oil you wish to use and spray the room in which you intend to meditate. If you want to enhance the effect, apply a few drops of diluted essential oil to your wrists.

If you're going to meditate in the bath, add a few drops of undiluted essential oil to your bathwater.

CANDLE MEDITATION

Some people like to focus on a candle, allowing their vision to blur and images or ideas to appear. The different coloured candles can enhance the meditation, as can perfumed candles.

Lie in a bath of scented water with the lights turned off and gaze at the candle flame. This can be a prelude to meditation, and it can calm the mind.

FLAME
MEDITATION

This is sometimes referred to as "fire gazing". This was well known in the days when most people heated their homes with open fires, but it isn't so familiar nowadays. To do this, you stare into the flames of a fire and let your mind drift into a trance-like state.

Some people may see images in the flames, while others can be inspired or find answers to problems.

WATER MEDITATION

Centuries ago, Nostradamus gazed into pools of water to see his visions. If you allow your mind to relax while fixing your eyes on a bowl of water, you might also see strange patterns or find yourself "knowing" about a specific situation. Others will visit the ocean and meditate to the sound of the waves.

SCRYING

This is like the water meditation opposite. It involves looking at a black plate or bowl and letting your mind drift. Ideas, thoughts, feelings about people or about the future may come, and in time visions may also occur.

This is similar to crystal ball gazing, which follows the same principle.

HERBS
and SCENTS

When choosing essential oils, consider the effect you would like them to have on you as well as the fragrance, as they each have specific qualities. Citrus, mint and eucalyptus are envigorating, lavender and rose are calming, while woody notes such as cinnamon and cedar are warming. Here are a few favourites.

CEDARWOOD

If you want to increase your spirituality, cedarwood can help to uplift and aid focus on your higher self while you meditate.

After the process, it would be a good idea to rest in bed, as this effect can continue for some time afterwards. You may notice that your dreams may be a little strange or highly colourful.

FRANKINCENSE

Frankincense is excellent for helping the memory, so this can keep the brain alert, especially if you have a busy life that has become somewhat overwhelming.

Medically, if a person is suffering from sinus problems, this can enable them to breathe more efficiently and to sleep more soundly.

LAVENDER

Lavender is one of the most potent relaxants of all. It has a soothing perfume and, if used on bed linen, it can bring a good night's sleep. If you have had a hectic day at work and you choose to meditate with this aroma, it should take the stress away, putting your mind into a more positive way of thinking.

MYRRH

This powerful aroma has several benefits in meditation, as it is excellent for de-stressing and helps the mind to focus clearly. It is particularly suitable for people in management who have many responsibilities and who find it hard to switch off when their work is done.

If this perfume is used with a guided meditation, it works very well.

ROSE

This essential oil is a great relaxant, and it can put you into a settled frame of mind. If you are doing a garden meditation, this will help to create the mood that you want.

Rose oil is very soothing, and it brings comfort and hope if you are downhearted.

SANDALWOOD

When a person becomes run down to the point where the brain is muddled, sandalwood is believed to be helpful.

In Chinese medicine, this oil is revered for helping anxiety and depression.

When using it in your meditation, focus on your breathing technique and allow the aroma to banish negativity and bring optimism in its place.

YLANG YLANG

This has a beautiful aroma and has been used by top perfumers from all over the world. If a person is sad or is suffering grief as a result of losing someone dear to them, it can be hard to elevate their mood.

Ylang ylang essential oil helps to restore optimism, banish anger and relieve the emotions of mourning and stress.

CHAPTER

8

CRYSTAL
MEDITATION

Using crystals with meditation
is fast becoming popular.
The vibrational frequencies of each
different stone encourage the soul to
experience different moods, which
influence the way we think and feel.

An easy way to do a crystal
meditation is to sit or lie comfortably,
holding the crystal of your choice.
If you have a specific problem in
your life, you can go online or visit a
crystal shop and search for a stone
that corresponds to your issues.
Hold the chosen crystal throughout
your meditation to gain
empowerment and clarity.

"Be the energy you want others to absorb."

A. D. Posey

AMETHYST

If you are not feeling well, amethyst would be a good healing crystal, and it can also soothe a troubled mind. It is said to be helpful after surgery or prolonged illness, too, as it can restore energy patterns.

Many people keep a piece of amethyst by the bedside to ensure a good night's sleep.

ROSE QUARTZ

Perhaps you are lonely and would like to have a loving relationship or a companion by your side with whom to share your life.

When holding this delicate, pink crystal, concentrate your meditation on finding your beloved. During your meditation, envisage your perfect partner holding your hand, and take an imaginary walk with them to somewhere beautiful.

TURQUISE

Sometimes life makes us feel unprotected, especially if you live in a rough neighbourhood or have spiteful people around you at work.

Meditating with this powerful stone should help you to feel more empowered, and it will protect you from life's complications. This stone can also help you to find answers to problems, as it can bring clarity to your mind.

TIGER'S EYE

If you are in a situation where you need courage, this crystal will help you to find it. Meditate with a piece of tiger's eye in your hand, focusing on your problem and imagining yourself having the courage to stand up to whatever is opposing you. Imagine your troubles being put into bags and sent out into the universe, far away from you and your loved ones.

CHAPTER
9

MEDITATING

with

NATURE

In folklore, it was said that if you had a problem you needed to solve, you should find an old oak tree, sit with your back against the trunk and allow the wisdom of the tree to guide your mind in the correct direction.

This can work exceptionally well if you have decisions to make. Ensure your back is hard against the tree and place both hands on the ground. Close your eyes and feel the energy of the roots beneath you. Clear your mind and silently ask the tree to help you. People often report having feelings of wellbeing after meditating this way.

Another old belief is that carrying a few oak leaves in your pocket may help if you suffer from a heart problem. However, you must still take your heart medicine and follow all your doctor's instructions; never rely on the oak leaf therapy alone!

MOON MEDITATION

Most of us believe in the magic of the moon and will often gaze up at its beauty. Pagans, witches and Druids worship the lunar cycles and will speak to the moon for protection and favours.

Meditating under the moon is a powerful therapy, and it can alter a person's consciousness.

On a clear, dry night, place a blanket on the ground or put a chair outside and sit underneath the moon. Perform your usual breathing meditation for around fifteen minutes.

Pay attention to how you are feeling while you bathe in its light. You will emerge refreshed and renewed.

BIRDSONG MEDITATION

If you have a garden, then, when the weather is pleasant, sit or lie on the grass and meditate for around fifteen minutes on the sound of the birds.

This kind of meditation can really resonate with the soul, connecting you to the power of nature and the animal kingdom.

"Nature does not hurry, yet everything is accomplished."

Lao Tzu

CLOUD MEDITATION

Cloud meditation comes naturally to most of us, and it can be very liberating. You can do this in the garden or in a private beauty spot that you may have discovered. Lie on your back and see if you can make out any images from the clouds.

This practice is soothing and allows the mind to wander positively and creatively. You might even be able to see shapes that lead on to clairvoyance and the ability to see into the future.

RAIN MEDITATION

There are those among us who believe in the power of weather, and if you don't mind getting wet, you might like to meditate in the pouring rain and connect with Mother Earth.

When meditating this way, the rain will cleanse and invigorate you, but be sensible and don't stay outside too long if it's cold.

STARLIGHT MEDITATION

Many people will take a tent and go somewhere remote in the hope of connecting with the universe. On a clear night, lie down on the ground, keep your eyes open and marvel at the stars overhead.

Those who believe in aliens and otherworldly entities will try to link into extraterrestrial energy this way.

"If you are quiet enough, you will hear the flow of the universe. You will feel its rhythm. Go with this flow. Happiness lies ahead. Meditation is key."

Buddha

CHAPTER
10

MEDITATION
for the
SOUL

This is your time, because meditation is a very personal experience, and it is perfectly acceptable to be self-centred. This is about you, your body and your knowledge of what is happening to you. You can return to this meditative place of safety whenever you want to, especially if you find it hard to sleep or relax.

Many people use spiritual meditation to elevate their consciousness and to work out their own problems. This is now becoming widespread around the world, and many people are seeking their own perception of truth.

A lovely mantra to repeat is:

*"Nobody wants
anything;
nobody needs
anything;
I can be me,
I am free!"*

CHILDREN'S MEDITATION

If you are a parent, why not try to teach your children to meditate? They usually take to it like ducks to water, and it will stand them in good stead in the future.

Create a guided journey for them so they can meet unicorns and fairies or a favourite animal they would love to be with. It also helps to have gentle music playing.

BEDSIDE MEDITATION

Small children sometimes have night terrors, and a simple meditation can help to get them back to sleep. Tell your child to close their eyes and imagine a favourite toy coming to life. Hold their hand and take them on a beautiful journey through some fairy-tale scenery.

You could also tell them that the toy will be watching over them as they sleep to keep them safe.

HOW TO MEET A LOVED ONE WHO HAS DIED

- Make yourself comfortable and relaxed, using breathing techniques.

- Visualize yourself standing at the base of a high green mountain that is shrouded in a low, misty cloud.

- A gentle pathway curves up the side of the mountain, and you start to climb. Taking your time, you enjoy the feeling of power in your legs.

- As you ascend, look back and see your starting point below, then continue with your journey.

- At last, you see the top of the mountain and feel yourself being energized. You might experience a sense of anticipation and excitement.

- As you continue with your climb, feel yourself climbing through the tendrils of mist as you near the summit. The pinnacle is now in sight, and out of the mist, a figure starts walking towards you. You recognize this person and get a keen sense of knowing.

- If you meet up with a loved one who has passed over, you may notice they look younger than when you last saw them. This is normal, as they want you to know they are now well, healthy and happy.

- Finding a bench, you sit together and spend as much time as you want, talking to them and reminiscing about your lives together.

HOW TO MEET YOUR SPIRITUAL GUIDE

- If you wish to connect with your guide, the person you see in your vision may seem familiar as they approach.

- Greet the figure in any way that seems appropriate, and then ask the things you want to know, and take as long as you need to complete your visit.

- When you are ready, say your fond farewells and feel reassured that you know you can come back again at any time you wish.

- You start to slowly make your way back down the curving path and briefly turn around to see the person standing and waving affectionately as the figure gently disappears back into the mist.

- As you come back down the path, you see your starting point below and notice that you feel lighter and more energized than you did before.

- At a slow amble, you return to where you started and send a mental message of thanks to the figure you met.

FIND YOUR INNER SANCTUARY

- Imagine it is a warm sunny day, and that you are in the countryside enjoying a gentle stroll.

- You find yourself walking along a headland looking out to sea; the ocean is crystal blue, and it is calm and peaceful. In the distance, you spy a beautiful, private cove with golden sand. There is no-one on the beach, so you decide to go and explore.

- You find steps leading down to the beach and, taking hold of the firm handrail at your side, you gradually begin to descend. With each safe step you go down, you feel more and more relaxed.

- When you reach the bottom of the steps, you find yourself on golden, powdery sand.

- If you like, take off your shoes and feel the heat of the sand against the soles of your feet.

- Start to walk down to the shoreline.

- Notice that the weather is getting warmer without being too hot, and a gentle breeze lifts your hair.

- As you walk, you feel the sand becoming a little firmer beneath your feet; you realize that the tide is going out.

- Looking at the water, you see small wavelets, topped with frothy white seafoam, lapping up the sand, before quickly retreating. You can hear that soft swishing sound as the waves break on the beach, and you find this gentle rhythm so very hypnotic and relaxing.

- By now, you are at the water's edge and are strolling along the soft, wet sand.

- Look back at where you were and see the imprint of your footsteps in the damp sand.

- See the waves lapping up and filling the footprints, and then watch the water seep back in little rivulets into the ocean.

- This place is peaceful and restful, and as you continue your amble, you notice every detai: the sunlight shimmering on the waves and the tiny pieces of quartz in the sand sparkling like jewels.

- Breathe in the fresh air, relax and just enjoy the wonder of nature

- After a while, you feel tired.

- You notice that there is a reclining sunbed under a parasol at the top of the beach.

- You decide to walk along the soft powdery sand and lie down on the sunbed; it feels so comfortable, warm, relaxing and safe.

- Just close your eyes briefly – it is a perfect moment in time for you. You will be in harmony with the world and find inner peace.

- Allow yourself to just be in the moment.

the THIRD-EYE MEDITATION

AJNA CHAKRA MEDITATION

This meditation is most effective while in a warm bath or just before bedtime. The third eye needs to be awakened, so first gently massage the area between the eyebrows for about a minute.

Lying on your back, close your eyes, focusing on the space between the eyebrows, and breathe in deeply to a count of three, and then breathe out slowly for a count of three.

Repeat this pattern for at least five minutes. Try to relax every part of your body until you begin to feel as if you are floating.

When the third eye starts to open, there may be a dull throbbing or heavy feeling where you have massaged your forehead.

Many people feel slightly giddy, but this is quite normal. Some say it can be alarming to open the third eye, as many new experiences may suddenly manifest themselves, so this technique is not for the faint-hearted.

Dreams could become bizarre or very colourful and vivid, and you might also experience sensitivity to light.

You will obtain new psychic knowledge, and your awareness will be more acute. Many people find they can read other people's minds or have premonitions of the future.

More experienced people might experience astral travel and develop an ability to travel to distant places.

IS THIS MEDITATION SAFE?

If you feel uncoordinated or slightly odd, this meditation might not be for you. Although it can't harm you, it can be a strange experience, and it doesn't suit everyone.

If you master the technique, you will find a better understanding of your place in the world and what your future should be. The decision is yours alone.

WHEN IT STARTS TO WORK

Stare through the third eye for five minutes or so and continue with the breathing process. Gradually, bright colours will float into your vision, like those seen in lava lamps. The colours are usually purple, red, blue and yellow, and they seem to fill the whole of the forehead.

Reaching this stage feels terrific, and it shows you have succeeded in opening the third eye.

WHAT HAPPENS NEXT?

As the colours continue to blend, there is usually a great feeling of peace and wellbeing.

If you have been suffering any kind of physical pain, this may subside and become more bearable. Ask the universe for the things you need to make your life easier, or maybe ask for someone else's life to be made better.

*"We are shaped by
our thoughts; we
become what we think.
When the mind
is pure, joy follows
like a shadow that
never leaves."*

Buddha

CHAPTER

11

other
INTERESTING
TECHNIQUES

Power animals or totem animals are classed as spiritual guides who protect us, and they are said to help us throughout our lives.

Many psychics connect with their chosen animals via dreams for the information they can give us. Shamanic believers will travel in trance to meet their totem animals on the astral plane.

"*Be still and the earth will speak to you.*"

Navajo proverb

WHAT ARE THEY FOR?

A power animal's primary purpose is to guard their person against danger and to communicate spiritual knowledge to them. You cannot select the kind of creature you want, as that has already been done by a higher power.

So, while you might fancy a more fascinating creature than the one you have, that is just too bad. You may fear or dislike certain animals, but it is precisely that animal which may be your power animal. It may be that we need to conquer our fears or reach a better level of understanding of a specific species.

During meditation, you might envisage a creature like a bear, snake, wolf or cat, and if your animal happens to be a ferocious or fierce one, try not to be frightened. Each creature holds a positive power that it can relay to you. You might have an affinity with a particular type of animal and collect pictures or ornaments of that type, which means you are tuning into your animal on a psychic level.

Psychic people such as mediums and clairvoyants can sometimes see an individual's power animal standing beside them.

VISUAL MEDITATION

Sit or lie down comfortably with some gentle music playing and breathe in through the nose for a count of three and breathe out through the mouth for a count of three.

Focus on this rhythm for ten minutes, and when you feel ready, look through the third eye and ask mentally:

"Can I meet my power animal?"

The lava lamp colours begin to form, letting you know that the system is working. It will take a while to be successful, and it might even take a couple of weeks to master it, but don't give up because practice makes perfect.

Gradually the animal's face should appear in your vision.

Once you have a clear image of your power animal, you can summon it to protect you during every meditation you have in the future. Before you begin, silently call out to it to help you on your journey. See its face in your mind's eye and mentally embrace it.

Another way of finding a power animal is to meditate to the sound of rhythmic drumming, so you might want to download some Native American or African drumming for the purpose.

LUCID DREAMING

This is truly a unique experience because it involves you choosing to dream when you fall asleep, and then remembering your dreams. With practice, you may also be able to decide what to dream about. These next few pages show you how to go about it.

Lucid dreaming is fascinating, but it can be a little scary if you are unprepared, so you must practise the following steps to begin.

Start to use the MILD technique, which stands for Mnemonic Induction to Lucid Dreaming. Every night repeat this mantra:

"I will always be aware when I am dreaming"

and continue saying this until you fall asleep.

Practise reality checks within your dream. For example, glance at the page of a book and memorize some of the words.

Look away and then back to the page, and the text will not have changed, but if you are dreaming about the book, the version may vary significantly. Or look at a clock face, remember the time, turn away and turn back again. If the time is the same, it shows that you are awake and in the real world; if it differs from your recollection, you are dreaming.

Be prepared to experience sleep paralysis. This is a phenomenon where the body prevents physical movement during sleep, to prevent the sleeper from hurting himself as a result of a vivid dream.

If you feel worried about being unable to move, just remind yourself that you are doing this deliberately and it is part of your safe lucid dreaming practice.

Use a breathing technique to relax and see yourself going to sleep. Then, feel yourself becoming more aware of and more able to take control of your dream. Look for signs that you are dreaming, such as repeated and familiar images.

If you are not sure that you are dreaming, try one of the reality checks above, or do something you couldn't do in reality, such as walking through a wall or flying quickly into the air. It is important not to get over-excited when you are lucid dreaming, as you might inadvertently wake yourself up.

CHAPTER

12

SENSORY MEDITATION with COLOUR and TASTE

Use the three breaths in and three breaths out method and relax completely. Then, when you feel comfortable, imagine a vast rainbow. Remember the colours of the rainbow are red, orange, yellow, green, blue, indigo and violet.

By envisioning the colours of the rainbow, you can stimulate all your senses.

If you or someone you know is experiencing bad health, meditation can help the healing, and using different colours can enhance the process.

The brighter colours such as yellow and orange can lift depression, so bathing yourself in an imaginary circle of these colours can dispel negativity and lift the spirits.

RED

Feel enveloped in a glowing, red light. It is warm, safe and comforting, and it reminds you of long, happy summer days.

You are in a field with many happy people, and you are all picking strawberries. You can smell and taste the sweet flavours of each piece of fruit.

ORANGE

Move on and be surrounded by an orange light. It feels warm, but it is more vibrant than the red, and now the aroma and sharpness of oranges fill your mind.

This colour energizes you, and you may feel a gentle tingling sensation entering your body.

YELLOW

Again, when it feels right for you
to do so, merge yourself into the
yellow light and enjoy its vivid energy,
filling you with a new zest and
encouragement.

The vitality is stimulating, and the
smell and flavour of bright, yellow
lemons give you a real sense of
motivation and an urge to press on.

GREEN

Now feel yourself being enveloped in a bright green light, while the smell of freshly mown grass surrounds you. Luckily, hay fever sufferers will not be affected by these thoughts.

The sensation you experience changes to a more relaxed feeling. This is a time to chill out.

BLUE

Continuing the feeling of relaxation,
find yourself immersed in a beautiful,
pale blue light just like the colour of
the sea on a sunny day. The salty tang
of sea air reminds you of pleasant
holidays and gentler days of long ago.

The wonderfully fresh air raises
your spirits and makes you feel glad
to be alive.

INDIGO

Find yourself drifting into the indigo light; this continues to make you feel comfortable and relaxed.

The smell and taste of juicy plums fill your senses, and pleasant memories of the past remain. Awareness of impending completeness surrounds you as you continue your journey through the rainbow.

VIOLET

Find yourself enveloped in the violet light, reminiscent of the night sky as the last rays of the sunset appear and the time to rest and sleep arrive.

The scent of violets and lavender drift around you, helping you to feel comfortable and peaceful while this journey ends.

Other emotions

PINK

Pink stands for compassion, and
when using this colour in meditation,
it can show you that you need to
be more patient towards those
around you.

If you feel you can't cope with
someone's moods or demands,
envelope yourself in this
delicate shade.

Other emotions

RED

Red is a vibrant and compelling shade, as well as being dynamic, especially about business or romance. It gives courage and determination to succeed, even when the chips are down.

If you must attend an important interview, do a short meditation surrounding yourself in this colour to promote success. It can be useful to wear a red scarf.

Other emotions

YELLOW

Yellow is the colour of the sun,
without which there would be no life.
This is an excellent shade with which
to surround yourself in meditation, as
it lifts the spirits and brings optimism.

If you have been through a spell
of depression and can't shift those
black moods, sit for an hour in
the imagined glow, or even wear a
yellow scarf while you soak up this
healing colour.

Other emotions

GREEN

In folklore, green is known to
be a lucky colour, especially in the
form of a green four-leaf clover
or banknotes of the same shade.
When money is short, it can cause
significant worry and fear.

Sit comfortably and meditate on
being bathed in vibrant shades of
either lime or emerald green. Imagine
bank notes showering over you
and falling into your lap to
bring prosperity.

Other emotions

INDIGO

Many spiritual healers use an indigo
or violet flame to help someone
return to better health. Lie down and
use the third-eye technique
to visualize a beautiful, indigo colour
surrounding your body, and allow it
to permeate into your skin and
vital organs.

Indigo can heal past mistakes,
ease emotional pain and help you to
obtain closure on the past.

BLUE MEDITATION

There are many shades of blue, so choose one with which you feel most comfortable. The central theme of a blue meditation is protection. Sometimes, when things are going wrong, and you think that you are not in charge of your life, this shade will help to dispel hopelessness and despair.

For instance, you may be suffering from being bullied in the workplace, or you might have a violent situation going on around you.

the METHOD for
BLUE MEDITATION

Find a quiet place to sit or go into the garden if you have one. Close your eyes and breathe regularly, while imagining the colour blue flooding into your diaphragm area. Gently, move the colour upwards to the throat, nasal passages, the forehead and crown chakra.

Sit still for ten minutes and breathe in the colour to remove negativity.

WHITE MEDITATION

If you want to become more spiritual and enlightened, white is very helpful. This meditation is best done at bedtime, and make sure that phones and external noises are kept to a minimum.

Some people sleep with pets on their beds, so it would be better to put them in another room, as they can be distracting.

the METHOD for
WHITE MEDITATION

Start with the three breaths in and three breaths out meditation, deepening the breathing and keeping the rhythm steady. Focus on a spot between your eyebrows, and imagine white light entering this area and spreading through the forehead, the crown chakra and the throat and chest area. Bring the white colour into your arms, stomach, lower body, legs and feet.

Allow this beautiful white light to cleanse every part of your body, leaving you peaceful and revitalized.

a MEDITATION for WORLD PEACE

Sometimes, we may feel a need to link into the planet we live on and meditate for world peace and happiness. You may prefer to do this as part of group meditation because this is more powerful than meditating alone.

Still, either alone or with others, the mind can reach out to make a difference in what seems like a depressing situation.

"When things change inside you, things change around you."

Anonymous

"When you realize there is nothing lacking, the whole world belongs to you."

Lao Tzu

"Your body is precious. It is our vehicle for awakening. Treat it with care."

Buddha

CONCLUSION

One thing that's for sure is that meditation will open the door and the mind to new adventures and awareness. Yes, it does take time and discipline, and you will think: *"I'll never get the hang of this."* You may conclude that everyone is much better at doing this than you are – but they probably feel the same as you do. Don't lose heart. In time you will create your own way of practising, and there will be trigger points along the way to discovery and success.

It took me eighteen months to achieve a successful meditation, because my mind kept wandering to my shopping list and what to make for dinner, not to mention sometimes just falling fast asleep!

Noisy cars were speeding by and once the cat jumped on my lap, digging her claws into my knee, while the worst thing was the phone ringing because I hadn't taken it off the hook. In the end, I made a list and ticked off everything that I needed to shut down before I began.

I have also discovered that if you can do a meditation near running water, it is more powerful, but if you are going to do that kind of meditation, visit the bathroom first! I bought a little indoor fountain for water meditation, and it works perfectly. Still, you might decide to sit near a water feature in your garden and have the added magic of birdsong included.

Meditation takes time and practice, so don't give up at the first setback; just start by going to bed thirty minutes earlier than usual and try to stay awake.

Someone once told me that ten minutes of meditation is equivalent to two hours of sleep, so bear that comforting thought in mind.

Remember:

by the inch, it's a cinch, by the yard, it's hard!

"Meditation brings wisdom; lack of meditation leaves ignorance. Know well what leads you forward and what holds you back, and choose the path that leads to wisdom."

Buddha